Building

SCHOOL CULTURE

FROM THE INSIDE OUT

[An easy three step process
with immediate results]

JC POHL

WITH RYAN MCKERNAN

ISBN-13: 978-1540579461
ISBN-10: 1540579468

TEEN TRUTH is an educational services company focused on empowering student voice, enhancing school culture, and building student resilience. Developed from the success of an award-winning student-shot film series, TEEN TRUTH boasts North America's premiere motivational assemblies, leadership summits, and peer-to-peer curriculum.

Published by Horizon Intertainment, LLC

Dedications

JCP: This book is dedicated to my parents. Their lives spent as educators for over 30 years is what inspires my path today.

RM: This book is dedicated to the teachers and counselors who, when I wasn't sure which way to go, suggested I keep walking forward while I made up my mind.

Part One

Introduction
WHAT THIS TINY BOOK WILL DO

This tiny book offers a series of steps which you can take to quickly and easily reap the massive benefits of a positive school culture.

Some books do a fantastic job of explaining a handful of concepts over the course of hundreds of pages. In some cases, where concepts are illusive or complex, this can be a huge advantage. In others, it is an excellent waste of time.

Imagine, for example, that you are hosting a breakfast gathering. Your guests are eager to enjoy some pancakes, so you pull a cookbook off the shelf and get to work. If your cookbook went out of its way to describe the action of making those pancakes by describing each individual impulse of your nervous system while stirring, the muscle contractions required to crack an egg, the physics of the force generated behind flipping a pancake, and the ongoing chemistry of the entire process, it might make for an interesting read... but it would probably be a long time before you finally got those delicious disks of golden brown goodness onto the table. Unless you happened to be hosting a collection of very enthusiastic academics, that particular cookbook might not be the best option for your purposes.

[
This book contains a collection of concepts which are very easy to understand. Specifically, it contains three powerful but simple ideas that virtually any school leader can grasp and implement immediately.
]

The objective of this book is to help you build positive school culture from the inside out, and it contains a collection of easy to understand concepts that focus on that objective. Specifically, it contains three powerful but simple ideas that virtually any school leader can grasp and implement immediately. It would be silly to drag these concepts out to 300 pages, especially since I'm painfully aware of how many schedule demands you have.

Through my work building both TEEN TRUTH and RISING UP, I've seen schools around the world and I know there is one thing all of you have in common: you pour a lot of your own time into your schools, and as a busy executive myself I understand how important it is to get things done efficiently.

This book will cover topics quickly, so that you can comfortably get through each of them as you enjoy breakfast, lunch, and dinner throughout a single day. It will also offer a concrete process through which you can implement these ideas, and apply them to your school. These actions will have an immediate, positive impact on your school's culture.

Fortunately in this case the workload is actually quite light, and the benefits are tremendous. To illustrate, filling the "bucket" of school culture one drop at a time is difficult, but bringing the bucket to a water source and turning on a faucet takes much less effort by comparison, and creates a continuous benefit. With this book, I hope to show you a few of those water sources, so you can fill your school's culture bucket, and save yourself a whole lot of time and stress while doing so.

But first, let's make sure we understand this bucket we're filling.

What is School Culture,
AND WHY IS IT IMPORTANT?

School culture is the collective manifestation of the attitudes, outlooks, and behaviors of the entire student, administrative, and faculty body.

It's what gives a school its own unique feeling as you walk through the halls. Are kids joking, smiling, and optimistic? Are teachers happy to see each other and excited about their day? Or is there a cloud of nervousness, negativity, and hostility hanging over everyone?

It can be hard to articulate exactly why we feel a certain way when we're in our school because it's often a collection of small cues, but it is very important to take notice. Environment - especially our social environment - plays a big part in how we feel. And how we feel within those environments has a massive impact on things like performance, decision making, and our outlook for the future.

Fortunately we can influence this aspect of our lives, and increase the likelihood of success and happiness by harnessing this powerful force.

[
Environment - especially our
social environment - plays
a big part in how we feel.
]

Imagine for a moment that your school is a sailboat, and you'd like to steer it toward the Sea of Success. In this analogy, school culture is the wind. If you ignore the wind, or try to operate against it, you may have a hard time getting where you want to go, but if you learn to understand and harness the wind, you can use it to drive the ship on a smooth and steady course.

If you'd like to see an example of how a shift in culture can result in big changes, take a look at Alan Mulally, the former CEO of Ford Motor

Company who turned the company around at one of its lowest points. During an era when the automotive industry was desperate for government bailouts, Mulally took Ford from a projected seventeen million dollar loss to being the only American automotive company that did not require a government bailout. Mulally attributes this to a change in culture.

Upon entering Ford, Mulally realized the company was fractured with several silos managing their own sections independently. He unified them by promoting a culture based around unity, resilience, and cooperation. So how can we do what he did? What was step one?

For Mulally, it started with a simple motto, "One Ford."

Action One

ONE FORD

ONE TEAM • ONE PLAN • ONE GOA

The Motto

I met Ryan Bellflower several years ago when he was still in high school. Ryan has a learning challenge, and kids sometimes picked on him in middle school because he was different.

But while he was in high school, some of the students on Ryan's campus decided to do something incredible. Instead of knocking him down or taunting him, they included him. Instead of hurting his feelings, they encouraged him.

With this newfound support, Ryan developed a profound interest in sports. And he decided to try out for the basketball team in his junior year. Some people told him he'd never make the team, insisting he just wasn't ever going to be able to keep up with the fast moving game.

That year, he got cut from the team. But the coach got in touch with him afterward, and offered him a position on the team as the manager. And Ryan's friends supported him, and they included him when they practiced.

The next year, Ryan earned his team uniform.

On the last home game of the season during his senior year, the players on his team - those same players who had supported him from the beginning - went to their coach and said, "We want Ryan in the game."

In that final game, with just ten seconds left, Ryan caught a pass from one of his teammates, and he threw up his shot just as time was running out. Everyone held their breath as the ball flew through the air.

And he sank a perfect shot - nothing but net!

> This is a prime example of how a motto can be one of the most powerful tools in your cultural toolbox.

It might seem unbelievable that something as simple as a motto could be the start of a complete social turnaround, but this is a prime example of how a motto can be one of the most powerful tools in your cultural toolbox. Here's how:

Jeff Eben is a fantastic leader in public education and a respected friend of mine. He develops positive school culture wherever he goes, and the backbone of his message is a simple motto, "Feel the Love."

The philosophy echoes up and down every school he visits, even years after he speaks there. You can hear it in the halls, bouncing between peers, being passed with a smile from a teacher to a student or vice versa. The most interesting part is, when you're in a school with Jeff Eben's motto, you really do start to feel the love.

It was that same motto that encouraged Ryan's school to support him. It was that simple statement that empowered him to seize his big moment. "Feel the Love" was the rallying cry of the teammates who stood behind, and believed in, Ryan Bellflower. You see, Jeff Eben was Ryan's principal. And it was his motto of "Feel the Love" that inspired those players to step up and become a positive force for their school.

There's no denying it, a motto is a very powerful cultural starting point.

So why do some mottos stick and have a tremendous impact while others don't? According to "Made to Stick" by Chip & Dan Heath, the difference between a motto that catches on and a motto that ends up being forgotten is simplicity.

Let's look at some of the mottos we all know.

- "Don't Mess with Texas"
- "Just Do It"
- "Protect this House"
- "Be All That You Can Be"
- "I'm Lovin' It"

What do these mottos have in common? Each of them have three important qualities. They are simple, direct, and positive. These three factors serve as a strong guideline for developing a motto. Let's elaborate on each point.

Keep it Simple

Don't use a five dollar word when a ten cent word will do. If your message is simple, it's more likely to be remembered, and much more likely to be repeated. We all have a lot on our plate, and we can only dedicate so much brain power to any single thing. We can easily remember and apply phrases like, "Just do it!" but struggle to recall a phrase like, "Simply engage in your intended action immediately!"

Imagine if that had been Nike's slogan! I don't think it would have caught on.

Make it Direct

The best mottos tend to have just one direct message. If we try to pack too much into a motto, then it becomes too complicated and we run into a problem similar to the one above. The phrase becomes overwhelming, more difficult to remember, and therefore less likely to be applied and repeated.

So instead of creating something like, "Be kind, respectful, courteous, and caring to each other," try to find a phrase that packs all of those ideals into a single thought. Maybe something like, "Be excellent to each other."

Another key point to this aspect of developing a motto is that your administration and faculty will naturally begin to focus their efforts on this particular point. This can be helpful when trying to resolve a particular problem. If, for example, your school has an issue with teasing, a motto like "Kindness is courage" will help to highlight the issue. Raising awareness is an important part of resolving problems.

Think Positive

A school motto should focus on the positive as much as possible because some students may use a motto as a way of harming one another if it is based on negative language. It's easy to imagine how a motto like, "Don't be a jerk" could quickly turn into an extremely negative force. What may have started out as a well-intended reminder not to be mean to each other could be hijacked and used as a trump card in arguments, or thrown at peers in a hostile and accusatory way.

> We can accomplish far more when we focus on our strengths than when we focus on our weaknesses.

Instead of saying a negative motto like the one above, use something like "Be someone's hero!" It would be much harder to use such a phrase in an inflammatory way, and as such will be a stronger source of positivity.

As a counselor and therapist I have seen the difference that can be made by focusing on the positive. Clients often want to focus on their problems, which is completely understandable. But when I can move the conversation to their strengths and inspire them to think of solutions, everything in their life starts to change. We can accomplish far more when we focus on our strengths than when we focus on our weaknesses. Your school's culture is no different. Think positively with your motto and everything will build from there.

Assignment One:
CREATE A MOTTO FOR YOUR SCHOOL

The above guidelines will assist in creating your own school motto! Maybe this is something you'd like to do yourself, or maybe it's something you'd like students and faculty to participate in. Students are an amazing source of creativity, and getting the student body involved will help them to "own" the motto. Teachers are also excellent candidates as a starting point for a motto, because they generally have a strong understanding of the big issues which the school should be focusing on, and can provide insight into what the motto should be about.

Whatever the case may be, make sure to follow the above guidelines, and encourage staff and students to use the motto regularly. Put it in plain sight, plaster it on every wall, add it to your morning announcements, and use it as your own tagline at the end of your interactions.

If you're stuck, I've included a list of some motto examples below. Feel free to use any of them! The important thing to take away from this section is that you take the next step and implement your motto into your school.

- Announce your admirations
- Accentuate the positive
- Highlight success
- Be the change
- Honor above all
- Family first
- Tell your truth
- Thankfulness is happiness
- Be the difference

If you'd like even more inspiration, here's an excellent little website for you to check out from Supreme School Supply:
http://www.supremeschoolsupply.com/school-slogan-ideas/

As you prepare for each new year, it may be a good idea to revisit your school's changing needs and create a new motto. It's a good idea to form a small group to review your motto and decide if it is still in alignment with the direction toward which you'd like to steer your culture.

This concludes the first section. In case you ever need to look back for a reminder, here is quick a summary of what we went through that can be used to jog your memory in the future:

- School culture has a large impact on performance, outlook, and decision making.
- A motto can influence school culture.
- Mottos should be simple, direct and positive.
- Your assignment is to create and spread a motto for your school.

Action Two

School Activities

Who is in charge of your school's extra-curricular activities? Usually, it is the Activities Director or Student Council Advisor. Regardless of title, the person or persons in charge of school activities will be one of your school's greatest influencers of school culture.

If someone didn't pop into mind straight away when you read the title of this section, then your first step will be to select someone to take the lead on school activities. Your next step should be to empower this person. By giving them agency, and empowering them to take initiative in regards to school culture, you will be unlocking a fantastic opportunity for both the leader you've chosen and the school itself. You'll also be helping yourself by sharing the responsibility of building strong school culture. Encourage your student activity leader to do the same, because getting several people, including students and the community, involved can be a huge help to prevent any single person from becoming overburdened.

> [Activities create community, and they are a fantastic way to unify the student body.]

Activities create community, and they are a fantastic way to unify the student body. They're also a lot of fun! Unfortunately, activities without a strong objective can be ineffective. Before you know it, their positive effects "wear off." If you've ever experienced a motivational speaker, you know that many of them get you fired up... but only for a few days. In building school culture, we aren't interested in temporary boosts. We want long term, positive, behavioral changes! So how can we create activities that truly inspire and unite the school? How can we turn something fleeting into something that lasts? Just as we did in the first section, we're going to break down the school activity plan into three simple, applicable principles which will strengthen the results of your school's events.

Get Social

First of all, in order for school activities to act as a culture creating force, they must be social. Get people talking or playing or dancing together, and you'll see a much stronger impact on school culture.

Too often we see schools with activities that don't engage or promote any kind of communication or interaction. There's nothing wrong with time alone, and self reflection is an important part of life, but if your objective is to develop culture then it's best for your activities to have some sort of social aspect to them.

I'd like to clarify that by social, I don't necessarily mean giant parties or massive pep rallies. There are many ways for activities to have a social element to them. A prime example of something social that isn't a giant festival is a book club. In a book club, much time is spent reading independently, but it is also a social tool because it gets people talking! If your activity naturally lends itself to discussion and gets your students talking, then it is a social success! On the other hand, if the activity is inherently solitary or effectively keeps students in cliques, it might not be the best option to choose for our purposes.

For example, hosting a raffle probably won't have a powerful social impact because it doesn't encourage or necessitate any interaction. Maybe a few kids will discuss it, but for the most part students will be experiencing this particular activity independently. It would be better to instead host an event where people come together in a common space, or are encouraged to interact in a positive way. Perhaps, instead of a traditional raffle, you could pose a difficult question with no absolute answer and encourage students to discuss the issue and pick one answer or another by entering their name into one of two boxes (each representing one of the answers). Then you could pick one, or several name(s) from each answer box and have your raffle that way. That way, you can still have a fun raffle, but with a social twist!

Create an Emotional Impact

Another important aspect of a culture building activity is that it must be emotional. We tend to remember things that have an emotional impact on us. Furthermore, we tend to remember positive events better than negative events. We can use these facts to our advantage when planning activities.

[
We tend to remember
things that have an
emotional impact on us.
]

Creating an emotional impact isn't always easy, but a good way to get started is by asking yourself "What is important to our students?"

A day like "Wear a Silly Hat" day probably would not have a particularly powerful emotional impact. It may be fun, and could result in some laughs, but it's doubtful that many of your students would remember it a year, or even a few months from when it took place. On the other hand, if you hosted "Give a Compliment" day, you'd be more likely to see a cultural change because you would be encouraging students and staff to engage in a behavior which will prompt positive emotional responses. For many students, receiving a simple compliment may have a spectacular emotional impact. Something as simple as hearing a student or teacher tell them, "You have a wonderful smile," may stick with them for the rest of their lives.

We tend to express our emotions, both positive and negative, and extend them out to the people around us. So doing something that has a positive emotional impact will be carried forward and spread throughout the school. Have you ever experienced a time when you started the day off in an average mood, but then met someone with an infectiously positive attitude? Usually when that happens, we take on that positivity as well!

Consistently Schedule Activities

If someone decides they want to run a marathon, but that person only practices one time, they probably won't be particularly successful in their goal even if they practice extremely hard that one time. But if they practice consistently, and make their training part of their life, then they are almost certain to succeed.

Culture building activities are similar. Imagine a student activities leader who wants to build positive school culture, but only holds a single assembly to do it. Even if that assembly is fantastic, it probably won't be as successful as another leader who plans a culture-building activity every month.

Try not to think of an activity as an isolated, one-time event. Instead, create a goal and think of every activity you plan as a step toward it.

If culture building activities become something your school does regularly, you will see results in the same way that the marathon runner who practices diligently. Instead of viewing them as a "one and done" event, or a box on your checklist to check off, ask yourself how you can make school activities a permanent part of your school's culture.

Assignment Two:
BUILD A SCHOOL ACTIVITY SCHEDULE

Working with your student activity leader (and maybe even a group of student leaders), try to plan a year's worth of culture building activities that have a social and emotional focus. Be sure to use the above guidelines, and don't be afraid to tap into other people's creative wells. It's a lot more fun to work with someone (or a group of people) to come up with these activities.

It might seem overwhelming to plan an entire year at first, but don't worry, we've got some examples to get you started!

The examples you will see below come from our Difference Maker Summit, which is a student leadership driven, school culture focused workshop that we've designed to help schools create a clear, specific, workable blueprint for their student activities calendar.

Through our Difference Maker Summit, we've worked with students, teachers, parents, administrators, and counselors to come up with countless ideas for school activities that fit the bill of being emotional, social, and easy to tie together for an entire school year. Here are just a few examples:

Family Movie Night

At one of our Difference Maker Summits, we had a school tell us that one of their biggest problems was that the students didn't get enough time with their families. Kids felt really disconnected from their parents and siblings, and it was agreed that improving family ties would be a big step forward for everyone. One of the students suggested a Family Movie Night, where the school would set up a projector in the cafeteria and invite all of the school's families to come and watch movies together. We were extremely happy with the outcome: families that hadn't been spending much time together suddenly had an amazing opportunity to get together in a fun, low pressure environment. This event was particularly notable because the parents were given a chance to get involved in the school's culture.

Another thing I really like about this event is that it's easily repeatable. It's not hard to imagine a school hosting a family movie night every month! Can you imagine the impact an event like this could have if it brought people together several times throughout the year?

The Week of Kindness

I love this example because it's simple, costs nothing, and has a truly tremendous impact! It's one of the reasons we encourage activity planners to get students to help develop ideas. "What if we have a week," this particular student asked, "where we encourage kindness?" From that spark, a weeklong theme with a different goal for each day of the week was born!

The concepts for a Kindness Week do not need to be crazy or elaborate. Maybe for your Week of Kindness, Monday could be Tell Someone You Care day. On that day, you make it every student's mission to tell at least one person that they care about them. It may not seem like much, but trust me, after a week of positive little boosts, you will start to notice a constructive cultural change.

Mix It Up Day

For Mix It Up Day, students are encouraged to sit at a different place for lunch than they usually do. If you really want to go all out, make the day picnic themed by laying blankets down as an option for the students to use instead of tables. You'll be amazed at how many new friends are made with this simple idea!

Friend In a Jar

Have students select a random name from a jar and spend time getting to know that person. Or, better yet, give them an activity or task to do with their newfound friend.

Stress Free Day

As a surprise, select a day when no homework or tests will be given. Encourage students to make fun and social plans with their extra free time. Have teachers take some of the time from their classes to relax and interact with students in a fun discussion.

Cover Mirrors with "You Are Beautiful"

One of the schools attending our Difference Maker Summit voiced a concern about body image. A student mentioned that sometimes seeing a mirror made her stress out a little bit because she would be reminded of a pimple, or slightly messy hair. I think we can all remember those days!

So we all talked about the impact mirrors have on a person's self-image. They're a great tool, we agreed, but we wondered what it would look like if students were given a break from them. A student suggested that mirrors could be covered up for a day with a sign that read "You Are Beautiful" in big, colorful, friendly letters. It was a huge success.

The Feeling Box

The Feeling Box can be used all year long. Have a community box where people can write how they feel. Regularly lead groups that discuss these feelings and offer advice on coping with these feelings. Or perhaps add a column to your school's newspaper addressing "The Feeling Box." A lot of students are experiencing powerful emotions for the first time, and starting a discussion about those emotions can provide them with a chance to begin to understand them.

Unplug Day

One of the most effective activities I've ever witnessed was Unplug Day. For one day students were asked not to use cell phones, computers, or any other screen at all. At first, I was skeptical. I thought there was no way the students would go for it! I'm happy to say, I was wrong. It was truly amazing to see how students embraced the idea. By the end of the day, the school was buzzing with positive energy. It was as if the entire student body was rediscovering itself. It is now a regular occurrence at several of our Difference Maker Summit schools.

Alternative Pep Rally

Schools usually do a great job of celebrating their sports teams through pep rallies, but what about other groups? What if a pep rally were held for the theatre group? Or the debate team? Or chess club? Let's celebrate all of the cool things students are doing, instead of only focusing on a handful of them.

Speed Friending

Have students hop from friend to friend like they would if they were speed dating. Encourage students to try to find a common interest, or maybe offer them an interesting topic to discuss. I love this activity because it always results in new friends being made, and a lot of students walk away from it realizing that we all have much more in common than they could have ever imagined.

If you're still not sure how to go about creating activities and you'd like a guided workshop on activity planning and creation, be sure to check out our Difference Maker Summit, which creates a specific plan for your school based on your unique issues, and generates an activity blueprint for your entire year. You can learn more about the program at www.teentruth.net

Before we move on, I'd like to take a moment to extend my sincerest thanks to The California Association of Directors of Activities (CADA). CADA has helped countless programs across the country to create positive culture. They've been truly inspirational with their own work, and have offered ceaseless aid to the development of both my programs and myself as a speaker. They've been instrumental in developing the methods in this book, and I am so grateful for everything they have done for me, and for the communities they have touched.

This concludes the second section. In case you ever need to a quick reference, here is a summary of what we covered:

- Put someone (or a group) in charge of school activities and empower them!
- Activities that are social and emotional will have the greatest impact.
- Use your community to develop ideas for activities.
- Your assignment is to build a school activity schedule.

Action Three

Empower Student Voice

The third and final action that this book outlines will be empowering student voice.

All of our programs at TEEN TRUTH are ultimately centered around this particular goal. What we've found is this: when you empower students, give them a voice, and offer them the opportunity to step up and take ownership of their school, they respond in overwhelmingly positive ways. They rise to the occasion, and exceed expectations in virtually every aspect of life.

We all feel powerless sometimes, and when we're faced with new, overwhelming problems and unfamiliar situations, it's easy to get lost in that passive state of mind. We might even feel like life is kicking us around, and that we're at the mercy of fates beyond our control.

Put yourself in a student's shoes, for whom much of life is new and maybe a little scary. Remember what school was like for you, and how even small problems could feel overwhelming. Do you recall feeling lost? Or maybe it took some time to find your voice as a young person? It's easy to imagine how a student could fall into that powerless mindset when you put yourself in their position.

[
By empowering students and giving them a voice, they realize that they can make changes.
]

By empowering students and giving them a voice, they realize that they can make changes. They realize they have the power to do build a fantastic life for themselves, and they begin to realize that they can help others do the same. Just by giving them an opportunity to speak their mind and have their thoughts and words influence their school's culture, we can help students to realize that they aren't lost or powerless, but capable of greatness.

The reason empowering student voice works so well is the same reason Alan Mulally's shift in culture at Ford was so effective: it hands ownership over to the students. When you give someone ownership of their culture, and that person begins to see that they can make changes to improve the culture that they're a part of, the confidence to improve spreads throughout the rest of their lives. Furthermore, they begin to feel responsible for their school - they want their school to be amazing because now their school belongs to them, too. School changes from a place they have to go to into a tight-knit community.

So what can we do to empower student voice? There are several avenues you can take, but we'll be covering two excellent options, both of which are tried and true ways that we have used to produce fantastic results.

ASSEMBLIES

There are a lot of options for school assemblies. Some of them are amazing for developing school culture and empowering student voice, while others might have a much different focus and won't be particularly effective for developing positive culture.

So what's the difference between an assembly that focuses on empowering student voice and an assembly that doesn't? We've outlined three aspects of an effective assembly to determine which is which.

Who's Talking?

Assemblies focused on empowering student voice need to, at some point, get the students talking! It can be a lot of fun to listen to an expert speaker, and sure, we can benefit from them. However, if an assembly is meant to empower students and help them find their voice, then it should be clear that the focus isn't on the speaker, but on the students themselves. Although the speaker may be doing most of the talking, there should definitely be quite a bit of back and forth going on between the speaker and the students. They should be asking for the opinions of the student body, encouraging participation, and looking to the students themselves to voice both problems and solutions in regard to the topics that are being discussed.

Are These Your School's Issues?

An anti-bullying assembly can be a great thing, but what if a school doesn't have a problem with bullying? What if instead, that school is really struggling with self-esteem issues? Or poor attendance? Or bad choices?

Assemblies should be part of a premeditated plan designed to address issues specific to your school. There are many ways to improve school culture, but if an assembly isn't addressing an issue relevant to your school, then students will be less likely to engage. On the other hand, if the issue resonates with your school, you'll see plenty of ears perk up.

Will It Stick?

It's easy to ramble on for an hour about all of the problems in the world, and a speaker can fill up half a presentation with stories of how negative impacts affected them, or someone they know, but my question is: Will it stick?

I can remember a phenomenal speaker who spoke at my high school. He told us amazing stories that motivated and inspired us, but to this day I can't remember any of his lessons.

So will your assembly programs stick? Will they leave a legacy? Unfortunately, a lot of motivational speakers fade into the distance as time passes, but referring again to Chip and Dan Heath's "Made to Stick" we learn that a story that sticks must present something to the audience that is bigger than itself.

The traditional approach to motivational assemblies is simply not effective. What is effective is bringing a brand, a movement, or a message onto campus that is bigger than just one person. Something that has a true legacy behind it.

The goal of any school culture building assembly should be to present an issue, help the students to understand why it's an important issue to resolve, and then focus them on how they can make a difference. Raising awareness is great, but if your speaker isn't equally focused on motivating your student body toward a solution, then it probably isn't doing much to develop positive school culture.

[
Don't do for students
what they can do for
themselves.
]

Peer To Peer Programming

The second option for empowering student voice is likely the most powerful tool offered in this book. In fact, research has proven that students engaged in peer-to-peer programing go on to better school based outcomes and report feeling more connected to their school, to themselves, and to their peers.

One of the most important things I learned from my mentor and longtime educator, Kathleen Bethke was, "Don't do for students what they can do for themselves."

From that simple concept, we developed the RIS-ING UP: Coaching Program. The focus of this curriculum is extending guidance efforts across the entire school while adding the least amount of work to counselors, faculty, and administration as possible.

The way the program works is this: we collect a group of older students who teachers have selected as having strong leadership potential. We then take those students through a short course which educates them on several critical counseling tactics that can be quickly and easily applied to the rest of the student body. Finally, we send those students out to the younger classes, and empower them to educate their peers in resiliency, planning, and building strong relationships. All of which can be applied to create a greatly improved school culture.

We've found that peer-to-peer programming works extremely well. Younger students tend to look up to their older peers, and are therefore very likely to listen to, utilize, and share the teachings of them. It also offers an opportunity to put a positive label on the older students, (we use the term "coach"). By offering this label to these students, they become more likely to adopt the positive behaviors associated with the term.

If you are able to set up your own peer-to-peer program, then here are a few tips to get you started.

- Use responsible, older students to reach out to younger classes.
- Give your students very clear objectives for each session.
- Implement a program that has actual curriculum behind it.
- Make sure to have a strong focus on relationship building
- Be certain to give students a chance to offer feedback
- Get them on their feet, and get them moving! Students thrive on physical activity.

If you'd rather use our RISING UP curriculum, which is easily scheduled and implemented on campus by professionals trained specifically in peer-to-peer programming, you can learn more about what we offer at wwww.RisingUpCoaching.com

If you don't see RISING UP as a good solution for your school, but like the idea of a curriculum focused on empowering students, then please take a look at the following organizations.

- PLUS Program
- #iCanHelp
- Rachel's Challenge
- Link Crew

This concludes the third section. In case you ever need to look back for a reminder, here is quick a summary of what we went through that can be used to jog your memory in the future:

- Empower student voice to encourage them to have ownership of their school.
- Assemblies that focus on student voice should be a dialogue that directly engages your school's issues and will be remembered by students.
- Peer to peer programming is one of the most effective tools you can use.

Final Thoughts

The power of positive culture can be seen in almost every successful community. I learned this firsthand during my years working for the Walt Disney Company. Consider the fact that DisneyLand, an undeniably successful organization, never refers to the people who come to their park as "customers" or "patrons" or "clients." Instead they call them "guests." Consider how powerful that little nuance is, and how such a tiny change in perspective can inform a drastic difference in behavior. It impacts the park and, ultimately, the entire company. It's an easy change to make, but it's a part of a cultural identity that has proven to be one of the most effective in the world. This is the power of culture, and it's at your fingertips!

The momentum from these three little steps will build quickly. Students want to excel. They want to be amazing, to have a fantastic life, and to help others do the same. Sometimes it's hard for a young person to articulate that fact, but we've seen huge breakthroughs time and time again... and more often than not, it's the result of a shift to a more positive school culture. As an administrator, teacher, or educational leader it is your job to make this happen. It is your job to build culture on campus. Because students want to learn. They want to be part of an amazing culture. And they want to believe in themselves and those around them.

> As an administrator, teacher, or educational leader it is your job to make this happen. It is your job to build culture on campus.

In closing, let me leave you with one last example, an example that drives my passion every day. As I write this book the city of Chicago has recorded its 500th homicide of the year, a stat that sickens most of us. By way of comparison the city I live in, Austin, TX, has had just 24 homicides this year. I bring this up because that boy or that girl in Chicago who walks through one of the most dangerous neighborhoods in America with nothing but a backpack and a lunchbag wants to learn, wants to be at school, and craves a positive connection. It is up to the adults of the community to create an environment for each and every one of those students that will offer an opportunity to build self-efficacy and send them into the world to become empowered, successful, warm hearted human beings.

If you've enjoyed this book, and are interested in learning more about developing positive culture, be sure to connect at www.teentruth.net and www.risingupcoaching.com or you can connect directly at www.jcpohl.com

For more information email:
info@teentruth.net

Thank you for reading, and I wish you the best of luck as you build an amazing culture at your school!

School Culture Reflection Worksheet

*P*lease use the following worksheet pages to guide your thoughts on the topics discussed in this book or to inspire interactive discussions with administrators, teachers, parents, and students. There are many paths you can take to build school culture on campus, but these student-centered tools can help you to focus on building an effective, positive and engaging foundation. If you need help, or simply want to discuss some ideas, please do not hesitate to contact us. We are here to help you find success, and to build school culture on as many campuses as possible.

Initial Reflection:

What is School Culture?

What are the benefits of positive school culture?

If you could magically change your school's culture into its ideal version, what would that look like?

Do you have the support and resources to build the above vision which you described?

If not, why not?

Your Motto

What motto(s) do you already live by on your campus?

What would a new motto need to accomplish at your school? (List words/ideas)

There is a rule in the creative process, known as the "Rule of 10," which states that if you write down ten ideas, at least one of them will be good. Use the space below to come up with ten mottos as quickly as you can. There are no wrong answers here, just go for it!

Your Activities

Name one recent activity you held at your school.

_____

_____

_____

_____

_____

Was this activity social? How?

_____

_____

_____

_____

Was this activity emotional? How?

_____

_____

_____

_____

Did this activity benefit school culture? How?

Considering the book, what might you do differently for your next activity?

Your Assemblies

What was your most recent school assembly?

_____

_____

_____

_____

_____

Answer how strongly you agree or disagree with the following statements on a scale of 1 to 5, with 1 being "strongly disagree," 5 being "strongly agree."

	Strongly Disagree				Strongly Agree
The students were involved in this assembly...	1	2	3	4	5
The topic discussed was relevant to our students...	1	2	3	4	5
This assembly had a lasting impact on our students lives...	1	2	3	4	5
This assembly had a lasting impact on our school culture...	1	2	3	4	5

Considering what you have read. Would you have changed anything about the assembly? If so, what?

_____

_____

_____

_____

_____

_____

_____

Your Peer-to-Peer Efforts

Is there a peer-to-peer curriculum at your school? If so, what is the goal of this program?

_____

_____

_____

_____

_____

_____

_____

Is this curriculum social? How?

Is this curriculum emotional? How?

Is this curriculum helping to form relationships?
How?

With the reading in mind, is there any way you
could improve this program? If so, how?

Final Thoughts

What motto have you chosen for your school?

_____

_____

_____

_____

_____

_____

_____

_____

_____

Why will this motto be effective?

_____

_____

_____

_____

_____

_____

_____

_____

What student-centered activities have you planned for your school?

What type of assembly would you like to see on your campus?

What will you do to create or improve peer-to-peer curricula on your campus?

_____

_____

_____

_____

_____

_____

_____

_____

What results are you hoping to achieve through your new efforts and programs?

_____

_____

_____

_____

_____

_____

_____

_____

When and with whom will you meet to discuss the results of your programs? How will you determine their success or failure?

What did you appreciate about this exercise?

About The Authors

JC Pohl is a producer and speaker who has reached nearly 8 million people with his message of resilience and personal power.

His work with TEEN TRUTH has sent him around the world, inspiring students, educators, and parents to tell their truth, and be the difference. He has keynoted conferences for CADA, TASC, BOOST, NASC, LEAD, NCSA, ACE, Texas School Safety Center, and the PTA.

His RISING UP: Coaching Program has reached students across the country and consists of a peer-to-peer curriculum used by school counselors, the Texas Department of State Health Services, 21st Century ACE Centers, and Communities in Schools.

Pohl is a Licensed Marriage and Family Therapy Associate in the state of Texas. Currently. He offers counseling services through his private practice as well as through the Austin Center for Grief and Loss and Austin Divorce Recovery. He holds a Masters Degree in Professional Counseling from Texas State University, San Marcos. He is active in the Austin community and has sat on the board of the Austin AMFT.

You can find him on Facebook and LinkedIn or connect directly at www.jcpohl.com.

Ryan McKernan is a comedian, writer, and editor. He has written several plays and a musical, and is in the process of publishing his first novel, "The Extraordinary Tale of the Ordinary Daniel Bucket." Ryan resides in Austin, Texas where he spends a large portion of his time trying to decide whether or not he can tell the difference between gourmet and gas station coffee.

CPSIA information can be obtained
at www.ICGtesting.com
Printed in the USA
LVHW11s1615031018
592275LV00003B/520/P